NUMEROI

Numerology Easy

Discover the Numbers in Your Life and How to Apply Them in Your Destiny, Career, Relationships, Money and Future

Donald B. Grey

NUMEROLOGY MADE EASY

Bluesource And Friends

This book is brought to you by Bluesource And Friends, a happy book publishing company.

Our motto is **"Happiness Within Pages"**

We promise to deliver amazing value to readers with our books.

We also appreciate honest book reviews from our readers.

Connect with us on our Facebook page www.facebook.com/bluesourceandfriends and stay tuned to our latest book promotions and free giveaways.

NUMEROLOGY MADE EASY

© Copyright 2020 - All rights reserved.

The content contained within this book may not be reproduced, duplicated nor transmitted without direct written permission from the author or the publisher.

Under no circumstances will any blame or legal responsibility be held against the publisher, or author, for any damages, reparation, or monetary loss due to the information contained within this book, either directly or indirectly.

Legal Notice:

This book is copyright protected. It is only for personal use. You cannot amend, distribute, sell, use, quote or paraphrase any part, or the content within this book, without the consent of the author or publisher.

Disclaimer Notice:

Please note the information contained within this document is for educational and entertainment purposes only. All effort has been executed to present accurate, up-to-date, reliable, complete information. No warranties of any kind are declared or implied. Readers acknowledge that the author is not engaged in the rendering of legal, financial, medical or professional advice. The content within this book has been derived from various sources. Please consult a licensed professional before attempting any techniques outlined in this book.

NUMEROLOGY MADE EASY

By reading this document, the reader agrees that under no circumstances is the author responsible for any losses, direct or indirect, that are incurred as a result of the use of the information contained within this document, including, but not limited to, errors, omissions, or inaccuracies.

NUMEROLOGY MADE EASY

Table of Contents

Introduction to Numerology 6

Chapter 1: What Is Numerology? 16

   The Deeper Meaning Of Numerology 18

      What Can Numerology Be Used For? 27

   How to Use This Book 29

Chapter 2: Numbers and Nature 33

Chapter 3: The History of Numerology 38

   Pythagorean Numerology 40

   Pythagorean, Kabbalah, and Chaldean Numerology 42

Chapter 4: The Basics of Numerology 45

Chapter 5: The Meaning of Numbers 48

   The Meaning of the Numbers 1 - 9 52

      Master Numbers 59

Chapter 6: The Personality Numbers 64

   The Life Path Number 67

      The Destiny Number 70

      The Soul Number 73

      The Personality Number 74

NUMEROLOGY MADE EASY

The Birthday Number 75

Chapter 7: Karma and Karmic Debt......................77

Karmic Lessons 78

Karmic Debt....................................81

Chapter 8: Other Numbers in Your Numerology Chart 85

The Current Name Number............................85

Solving Your Number for Your Career 87

Finding Your Number for Luck 94

Solving Your Number for Your Relationships ...98

Solving Your Number for Your Home and Environment 104

Solving Your Number for Your Health............110

Chapter 9: Numerology Everyday........................115

Chapter 10: Developing Your Intuition................119

How to Strengthen Your Intuition 120

Conclusion 124

Bluesource And Friends 127

References......................................128

NUMEROLOGY MADE EASY

Introduction to Numerology

https://www.pexels.com/photo/lots-of-numbers-1314543/

There is a myth (or belief) that, once upon a time, a creator, or the proverbial "higher power", wanted to hide something very valuable from people until they were ready to receive it. An eagle offered to take it to the moon and a mole wanted to bury it deep in the earth. A swimmer wished to put it in the deepest part of the ocean. But the creator knew that no place on Earth was beyond the reach of the greedy hands of man. So, the creator decided to hide the truth *within* people. What was this elusive possession that could neither be hidden in the heavens nor the Earth? It was the truth that created our reality.

This perceived reality that we experience in daily life can be broken down into simpler elements. These elements take on the sequential and sometimes random permutations of numbers. That is where numerology comes in. Numerology is the study of numbers and the effects they have on your life. It also takes a look at how they may even govern certain outcomes of your life.

The argument among people who are skeptical of numerology is often that it cannot be scientifically verified. And there is undoubtedly truth in this statement. Although it is often referred to as a science, numerology technically has not been verified by quantifiable evidence. Irrefutable proof still remains elusive and probably will for a very long time to come. Indeed, many numerologists will themselves state that what they tell you when they give you readings is not definite. These readings certainly should not be taken as an inevitable prediction of your future or something that is set in stone.

Not everything that is true and that can add value to your life has to be proven or disproven by science. There are many scientific theories that have still yet to be quantifiably analyzed by scientific fields. There are countless examples of science being unable to fully describe or comprehend certain phenomena, ranging from quantum entanglement to the M-theory in the Mandela Effect.

Numerology may be strange and rather mind-boggling, but that does not make it incorrect. There might be a mystical relationship between a higher power or divine entity, numbers, and sequentially-coinciding events. Science has not necessarily proven this connection yet, but it is not able to find definitive proof to oppose this type of thought pattern or belief system, either.

In the collective knowledge of humanity, the rigorous methods of science are relatively new. Thousands of years ago, knowledge and wisdom were primarily transmitted through oral teachings and via stories and conversations. It was only later that symbols were created to express and to maintain knowledge. Although tradition was strong, knowledge, in this primal sense, was deeply connected to the movements of the stars, to the pulsing cycles of life and death, and to the natural laws of the universe. Also, human beings were regarded, like all other beings, to be part of this intricate web of life.

NUMEROLOGY MADE EASY

It is only within the last few hundred years that science has been trying to bring physical evidence to the universal laws that our forefathers had knowledge of on an intuitive level. (And it is still trying to catch up.) So, when we choose to explore different ways of thinking or different narratives than we have inherited from our ancestors, we are simply taking it upon ourselves to consciously change our realities. This allows us to apply different perspectives and to figure out what works in creating healthier and happier lives for ourselves. An example of this is modern medicine. In some circles, modern medicine, as the institution that it has become, has sometimes been condemned as disempowering and exploitative.

When choosing to explore different worldviews, one may need to consider alternative ways of organizing their realities in their minds. This is often a path that is adopted by people who have become disillusioned by the mainstream narratives that require us to pursue a linear way of thinking and sequential way of life. Maybe, by picking up this book, you are one of those people who realize that we create our own realities. Perhaps you think that the conventional narrative you employ when you conform to that tiresome norm of a 9-to-5 day job doing something you hate is no longer for you; or, maybe feeling obliged to buy the latest car

NUMEROLOGY MADE EASY

or mobile phone is something that no longer serves you.

If you are looking for ways of thinking that allow you to see beyond the stifling walls of modern society as we know it, there are many possibilities available to you. Today, we have more access to the traditions and methods used by cultures across the world than ever before. This is not to say that we have to explore all of them. This is a misconception that many of us have learned from post-colonial society and its attachment to acquiring information for its own sake.

This world, to which we often feel like we are enslaved, is dominated by the left-brain processes of people. Oftentimes, the tyrannical thoughts of our rational minds govern the way that we act. This can lead us to feel isolated, separated, and disconnected from the world at large, which, according to traditional wisdom, is merely an illusion. One of the greatest fundamental truths of the ancient healing arts is that we can choose to experience our lives as part of something larger than ourselves.

While seeing ourselves in this way - as a thread in the colorful fabric of life - was once the norm, today it takes courage and willingness to see through the predominant worldview that we are bombarded with by our institutions and the media. We have to feel the ancient fire of inner knowing burning within us and trust our hearts to guide us home.

Changing your mindset to become more aligned with the cosmos requires that you tap into the mysterious and magical energy that makes up everything in existence. There are many languages that can help us practice letting go of our incessant and fruitless mental chatter, expanding our awareness to become more present in our environment and abide by the energetic ebbs and flows of every moment. Each time we learn more of the vocabulary of palmistry or tarot, for example, we are opening a new door from the confinement of our minds to infinite possibilities.

Numerology is one of those languages that can help us see the world and our place within it with fresh eyes and an open heart. Doing so can help us find new ways of making choices that create a better life for ourselves and others.

The fact that you have picked up this book must mean that you have some sort of intuitive connection with numbers. It may be the case that you have noticed certain numbers recurring in your life, or perhaps you just have a hunch that there is something more to numbers than meets the eye. The harmony of numbers may be echoing in your soul, a memory embedded deep in your psyche of something more profound than the superficial promises offered by the beguiling glitter of the material world - or the silver tongue of the media luring us into the illusion of "forever" or "happily ever after" while the prevalence of depression and anxiety in society soar to unprecedented levels.

Throughout this book, you will see that the study of numerology is a way of understanding yourself, others, and the world. Mathematics has evolved in communities in Asia and Australia, from Africa to the Americas, leaving no continent untouched. It is a way of representing the most fundamental, simplest ingredient in the alchemy and creation of the universe: Numbers. In this sense, mathematics is a universal vocabulary that cuts through cultural and linguistic differences to represent the highest, yet simplest, truths of the universe.

On an abstract level, it is hoped that by the time you reach the end of this book, you will be kindling your own flame of intuition and self-trust in using numbers to help you make sense of your life. I hope that this journey into the surreal and awe-inspiring landscape of numbers will provide you with a different perspective of numerals as the beautiful raw materials that contain the infinite potential for creation. You should also gain a deeper knowledge of yourself by using some of the tools that are provided here.

Once we have taken a historical tour into the origins of the true essence of numbers and looked more closely at the meaning of numerology, you will be introduced to how to develop your own basic numerology chart. You will accomplish this by working out some of your own, personally-important numbers based on your birth date and name.

It may seem strange that you have a specific number that can help you to make more sense of your life. This number is grounded in a spectrum of other numerals as noted in the grand ballad of the universe, rather than as simple components in an irrelevant mental equation. You will see that the perspective offered by numerology is one that transcends the self and even your current lifetime. Finally, you will be able to find out how to develop your intuition.

This book is aimed at helping you gain practical, living experience using the power of numbers. It may, at first, seem like a confusing topic; indeed, numerology can be complex. An experienced numerologist can superimpose layers upon layers of depth in interpreting the meaning of the numbers that

NUMEROLOGY MADE EASY

are presented. Numerology can be as complicated or as simple as you would like it to be.

It is beyond the scope of this book to provide an in-depth exegesis on all aspects of this ancient art; to achieve this would require far more elaborate work. However, you will come to realize that even understanding the simplest building blocks of numerology can empower you to use numbers to redefine the narrative by which you live and, ultimately, start creating a better life for yourself. You can create a life with specific intentions. You will find ways to peer through these new doors into the infinite worlds of possibility for growth and healing. You will see for yourself that numbers can be powerful tools to aid in your growth and evolution.

By placing some of the basic principles of Pythagorean numerology in the context of a general theoretical background, you will begin to understand the potential that numbers have to guide you on your journey through life (if only you allow them to).

The fact is that we are bombarded by numbers every day. Whether they are in our daily schedules, prices of items at the store we frequent, forms we fill out, or on our taxes - numbers are all around us. They hit our subconscious minds and energetic bodies like shrapnel in a warzone.

Under the framework of numerology, these numbers all have a vibration or energy that inevitably impacts us whether we are aware of it or not. The choice you must make is this: Will you keep ignoring it or allow the numbers to reveal patterns and cycles in your life that can help you improve?

NUMEROLOGY MADE EASY

Chapter 1: What Is Numerology?

https://www.pexels.com/photo/woman-in-red-long-sleeve-writing-on-chalkboard-3769714/

When you think of numbers, you may have flashbacks of falling asleep in math class in front of a board full of, what seemed like, scrawls of a foreign language. You may remember getting that gut-wrenching F on your exam, or the feeling of dread knowing that math class was next on your class schedule.

With the current existing education system, it should not be a shock that more and more people are starting to experience a sinking feeling in their

NUMEROLOGY MADE EASY

stomachs when they hear the word *math*, or cringe when they have to do a calculation. Or, perhaps, you may just feel an honest, down-to-earth sense of boredom. No one can blame you. Even into our adult lives, numbers are often seen as a trial, an expense, or a demand of incomprehensible skill. Even though people may strongly dislike mathematics, numbers are used every single day. Nevertheless, many people do not appreciate them because they are associated with paying taxes, working out budgets, and performing other tedious tasks.

Despite our reservations about them, numbers are a part of a universal phenomenon that needs to be seen in a much different light. Indeed, both ancient mathematicians and modern-day thinkers alike had and have a passion for numbers. For some of us, this may be absolutely inconceivable. A lot of people may wonder how somebody could enjoy working with numbers. However, the enthusiasm some people have for them enable these individuals to see the purity of these symbols beyond the language of the mathematics we know from school. They can see an underlying beauty that cuts straight into the heart of the tapestry of the universe. (Since you are curious enough to explore the depths of numerology, you are probably quite interested in numbers yourself.)

The Deeper Meaning Of Numerology

https://www.pexels.com/photo/blue-blur-color-dark-932638/

The world from which numerology originated was very different from the one we all know of today. When looking back into its origin and history, one can see that it did not come from a single place or country. Rather, this ancient practice could be found across many cultures of the world. It evolved several lifetimes ago when it was considered normal to access the spirit world regularly. Diving into the supernatural and paranormal realms allowed people to find answers that could help them heal and discover deeper meanings for life itself.

However, before we get into the finer details of numerology, such as the quirks and qualities of the different cultures and the nuances of the various systems, let us take a closer look at what numerology actually is. Also, we will find out how it can be used by the likes of you and me. Numbers may be confusing, but understanding how these symbols influence our lives can change everything.

Although there may be slight differences in the precise character of numerology across cultures, one thing is consistent, and that is the idea that events are intrinsically related on a mystical level to numbers (Numerology Secrets, 2015). It is believed that the power of numbers can be harnessed intentionally to help us understand ourselves, others, and the universe at large.

Ducie (2015) defines numerology as a "science, psychology, and philosophy of numbers". She used the word "science" to describe the concrete way in which numerologists look at numbers, "psychology" to describe the process of looking into past patterns to help us manage our present and future, and

NUMEROLOGY MADE EASY

"philosophy" to refer to the theoretical perspective adopted by numerologists in seeing the world through numeric cycles.

When we speak about numerology as a philosophy, we also make reference to the specific vision of numbers, as you may have come to understand it by reading the introduction to this book. It refers to a comprehension of numbers as something much more intrinsic to who we are as energetic beings that are part of the whole. Apart from the complex phenomena in the universe that mathematics can help us understand, like black holes and gravity, numbers in their discrete, unassuming forms (that we learn about when we are toddlers) are seen by some numerologists to have their own energy signature and vibrations.

To talk about numbers at a more advanced and highly technical level, theoretical physics has shown us that everything is made up of atoms. Physical reality as we perceive it through our senses can be conceptually deconstructed into billions of atoms, although we can't experience it in this way. Each atom can be said to be a number - a unique numbered piece of a larger construction.

NUMEROLOGY MADE EASY

Now that we have a clearer view of how numbers appear to the eyes of the trained and experienced numerologist, let us take a detailed look at how they can be integrated into our lives in the most valuable way. A very big part of the philosophy that underpins numerology is being willing to recognize the cycles of numbers that happen in our daily lives. Most of us in this day and age enter into adulthood having a linear trajectory of our lives: We are born, go to school and possibly a university, make a living, and achieve the goals we have set for ourselves. This occurs all the while preparing for a happy, comfortable, and abundant future.

However, numerology and other such worldviews allow us to move into a lifestyle that works in harmony with the nature of different cycles. In this way, we can revisit themes or challenges that we are having so that we can gain a deeper understanding of them, at the meantime learning and growing from them. In the same way that seasons come and go at fairly regular intervals, we may, for example, notice a certain number making an appearance during significant times in our lives.

Being aware of how and when numbers show up in the context of what we are going through at the time and with what we are thinking, feeling, and are cognizant of in mind, helps us to identify ourselves as sacred beings on a collective path toward enlightenment. By looking at the unique patterns of numbers in our lives and using them to identify cycles, we provide the opportunity for our past to create a blueprint for our future, and illuminating it. And when we light the way to a better future, we become happier and more adept individuals.

Each number has a specific meaning that you can interpret in an intuitive and personal way. Looking at how you handled situations in the past and identifying lessons that you learned from these events can help you resolve similar challenges in the future. Doing this can also assist you in overcoming them so that you can complete the challenges you are actively facing with in this life. Or, rather, you can use them to create a deeper, more enriching experience of your current existence as you dig deeper into the potential of each and every precious moment.

If we can associate themes, patterns, and lessons with the appearance of certain numbers, we are paving the way for creating a life that is grounded upon the process of being present. We would be integrating ourselves in the flow of energy and nature that is such a fundamental, yet commonly ignored, part of our human experience. Instead of cutting off these extra realms or dimensions of our experience that are in alignment with spirit in the constant pursuit of success in the material world, we can choose to become one with them and learn from them in ways that can help with our evolution as sacred beings.

As much as we like to have control over our lives and environment in this postcolonial, modern-day, technocratic world, we can't deny the fact that nature is a force that has the power to extinguish us in a heartbeat. This has more control over us than we like to believe. The cycles of nature define our reality - even when we are not aware that they do. The rhythms of life and death, birth and decay, and the rise and fall of the sun and changes in the moon phases are the foundation upon which reality is based. The natural world, and ultimately our existence as a species, depends on the delicate harmony of nature. Whether we choose to be conscious of them, align with them, or use them to our advantage is a different story altogether.

To these natural cycles of the seasons and tides, numerologists would add the cycle of multiple numbers. The idea of considering numbers to be linked to the natural cycles likened to those of birth and death may seem foreign to many. To mathematics, it is often seen as a construct of the mind - a theoretical body of knowledge that has no place in the world of sunrises and weather systems. How can a mental fabrication be classified as natural? The more philosophically-minded might even ask whether mathematics is an objective truth at all. In the next chapter, we will explore the territory that numbers have in the natural world in greater depth.

In the introduction, we hinted at the idea that numerology introduces a scale of time and dimension into human existence that transcends the boundaries of this lifetime. To elaborate, it is widely held in many popular belief systems (not just in numerology), that a human soul incarnates into different bodies and forms many times in order to evolve and attain enlightenment. The idea is that, before we are born, we set specific intentions of what our purpose will be, what kind of individuals we will be, and what lessons we need to learn in order to grow as much as possible.

Numerology is regarded as a tool that can help us remember who we truly are and fulfill the goals we set for ourselves. Once we are aware of the powerful role they can play in helping us to do this, numbers start appearing in synchronicity with our experiences. We can interpret them intuitively (and by using a method and system that resonates with us) in order to find completion.

The final point to be made regarding the underlying philosophy of numerology is that it assumes that the numbers of our birth date and the letters of our name are imbibed with energies, frequencies, and meaning that we can choose to use to define the perspective from which we view ourselves, others, and the world in general. This can assist us in redefining our life's narrative and, in turn, lead us to heal and grow on a spiritual level.

Now that we have worked to gain a better understanding of the philosophical aspect of numerology, let us return to the description of numerology as a "science".

While science may be a useful analogy to describe certain aspects of numerology, it by no means implies that numerology is exact. Many qualities that we associate with science as the pursuit of verifiable evidence do not hold true for numerology. For starters, the specific nuances of each numerological system depend on the cultural context in which it arises. Thus, they do not reflect universal, objective truth.

NUMEROLOGY MADE EASY

Also, it is important to mention that being a good numerologist, to a large extent, means using and developing your intuitive skills to interpret numbers and make sense of whatever is going on in your life. That being said, numerology is a science in the sense that it applies a set of rules and methods in order to better understand ourselves and the world.

Many people go to a numerologist with the high expectation of having the meaning of life bestowed upon them as a long-awaited solution to all of their problems. They believe it is the final destination for all of their suffering. They believe that once the answers have been revealed, they will be able to shrug their cares away and feel like they are sitting next to a glowing fire, whilst caught up in the storm of adversity.

However, numerology is best used in the form of a process that we can integrate into our everyday lives. Like any form of comfort we may take when we are challenged, staying in our comfort zone for too long can be dangerous. Also, trusting someone else to give meaning to your own experiences in a single numerological chart can be disempowering.

In the same way that leaving the fire to go back out into the storm takes courage and a little discomfort, trusting our own intuition can be difficult. We must put faith in ourselves to receive what are sometimes unexpected messages from the numbers we see in cycles in our everyday lives, not to mention taking in their lessons without judgment. This demands that we practice a little trust in the process of the universe and in ourselves.

What Can Numerology Be Used For?

So now you know what numbers are in the context of numerology. Let us take a look at the ways in which they can help guide you in your life. We have established that numerology is not a one-off event. What does this mean in terms of how you can apply it in your day-to-day life? Well, once you are aware of the significant patterns and numbers in your life, you can use them on a daily basis to help you navigate your present and future.

Numerology is often referred to as providing a "blueprint" for your life in the sense that you can project your future based on the descriptions provided on your readings. Of course, it should not be regarded as fortune-telling or prophecy in the sense that it cannot predict the course that your future will take.

You always have a choice. If we feel like we are being consumed by the dark night of mental confusion, the birth-child of a long history of analytical, critical thought can help illuminate new opportunities. It can show us fresh ways of seeing things. It is not to say that it is necessarily offering you a "life rope", but it offers, at the very least, a different way of viewing yourself from which you can learn more about yourself in different terms.

So, in essence, numerology can help you gain a greater degree of self-knowledge. Once you become aware of the patterns of numbers that occur in your life, you can use these symbols to gain a broader perspective of who you are and what your purpose is, as well as work through cycles that are continuing to repeat themselves in your current challenges.

The potential for numerology to help us in our everyday lives is immeasurable. First of all, the idea behind numerology is that numbers can help us better understand ourselves and others. It can provide us with a broader perspective of our soul's purpose in this lifetime so that we can approach everything we do from the heart space, rather than being directed by our inflexible minds.

Numerology helps us look into the past to notice the dates of significant events in our lives and see patterns and cycles that can help us maneuver more effortlessly through challenges we might face in the future.

How to Use This Book

Once we have gone into more detail regarding the place of numbers in nature and have covered the historical background of numerology, we will start exploring, on a more practical level, some of the basic numbers that feature on a numerology chart. You will then be able to see how this can be applied in your life. Although it is beyond the scope of this book to enter into a complete detailed account of the numbers that feature on a numerology chart, it aims to equip you with the know-how to work out five of the most essential and commonly-used numbers that are used by numerologists today.

NUMEROLOGY MADE EASY

You will be able to interpret them according to the teachings of numerologist and author Michele Buchanan's perspective and work out your own personal karmic patterns. You will become familiar with some of the other numbers that can be worked out. You will also gain a general sense of the ways in which you can dance with numbers that feature in your life to bring about change with intention.

We have touched upon the fact that the systems and methods employed in numerology tend to differ slightly from one another. Modern numerology is no different from the ancient version in the sense that they have their own nuances based on differences in tradition. The method used in this book is based on Pythagorean numerology; the interpretation of the respective numbers are based on the work of Michele Buchanan.

You may find that Pythagorean numerology does not resonate with you, and neither does the insight offered by Buchanan. If this is the case, don't be disheartened; the perspective offered in this book is only one of many, and you should take the time to find a system that makes sense to you. Understanding numerology is ultimately a personal journey, but once you have found something that works for you, stick with it!

NUMEROLOGY MADE EASY

The next chapter will briefly describe the profound presence that numbers have in the natural world in order to help you understand why numbers are regarded by numerologists as one of the fundamental cycles in nature. They truly can help us to see that our lives are in harmony with the music of the universe. Following that, we will take a glimpse at the origins of numerology and how it affects its practice today. After that, you will find out the basic principles behind Pythagorean numerology, as well as the method for working out your own numbers using this system.

Buchanan distinguishes between "personality numbers" and "forecasting numbers", where the former describes who we are and our greater soul purpose in this lifetime, and the latter helps paint a general idea of what we can expect to experience in this life. We will focus mainly on five of the personality numbers in this book, but we will also briefly touch upon the forecasting numbers that form part of a numerology chart. This way, you can get a more comprehensive idea of what a complete chart should look like.

The final chapters deal with more practical tips about the numbers that are present in our lives and how you can use them to steer your choices into creating the existence that you desire. We have suggested that numerology is, to some extent, an intuitive art. The final chapter will help you learn ways of developing your natural intuitive capacity.

In this chapter, you have become more deeply acquainted with what numerology is in a general sense, and you have been exposed to a perspective of numbers that you may not previously have been acquainted with. At this point, you should have a vague understanding of the significance of numbers in nature, cycles, and numerology. Even the best of us do not pay close attention to the presence of numbers in nature, but you will see in the next chapter that they are hard to miss when you look closely.

We will now explore some of the ways in which numbers take center stage in the natural world.

Chapter 2: Numbers and Nature

https://www.pexels.com/photo/environment-forest-grass-leaves-142497/

From hexagonal honeycombs to Newton's laws of gravity, numbers are everywhere in nature. However, in our busy 21st-century lives, we often take numbers for granted. Although they are found in all places, they often remain unseen. They are usually neglected like an abandoned car at the scrapyard begging for someone's attention and to be brought back to life. Once we can recognize the simple beauty in the presence of numbers in nature, we can start to allow these symbols to animate our world in ways we could never have imagined.

The first step in understanding the basic philosophy of numerology is recognizing the potential for adopting a worldview that is nonlinear and in alignment with the "random" cycles of nature. The second step is to make what may seem like quite a dramatic association between numbers and natural cycles.

In the framework of the typical education system that most of us are exposed to, numbers seem to be seen as functional commodities that we use to achieve certain things or to manage our everyday lives. At this point in the book, though, you may already be seeing numbers in a deeper way.

Mathematics is a language that humans have created to describe the behavior or patterns of numbers. It is necessary for us to gain a greater understanding of them and the structure of the universe. As the fruits of the imagination and passion of truth-seekers since the beginning of time, science and mathematics have taken us from knowing how to count to understanding more about the far reaches of the galaxy.

NUMEROLOGY MADE EASY

These sojourns into the unknown have continued to leave us awestruck as we reel from the beauty of the imagery we receive through the latest technology. But we don't have to travel far to see the beauty of numbers in nature. We can look at a flower, a snail, or an apple to find what is known as the "Fibonacci sequence", and it describes an elegant, energy-efficient system that governs much of nature.

This sequence represents the most commonly-occurring numbers in nature. It consists of the following numbers, ad infinitum:

1   1   2   3   5   8   13   21   34   55   89   144

The most obvious place to find evidence of this pattern is to look into the world of plants. The number of petals on a flower, for example, is usually one of the numbers in the Fibonacci sequence. Likewise, cutting an apple open will reveal five seeds; a banana has three. To refer to another example, the number of seeds in a row on a sunflower is a Fibonacci number.

The beauty of this sequence lies in more than just a set of random numbers. You may have learned the basic math of the Fibonacci sequence at school. Perhaps you have come to understand the special relationships that these numbers have to one another. For starters, each number in the sequence is the sum of the previous two numbers. Here is an example:

$$(1 + 1 = 2) \ (2 + 3 = 5) \ (5 + 8 = 13) \ (21 + 34 = 55)$$
$$(55 + 89 = 144) \ ...$$

What's more, if you divide each number by the one that comes before it (especially the larger numbers), the quotient is usually 1.618. In ancient Greece, this number was called "phi", though today it is more popularly known as "the golden ratio". It appears in various contexts in nature, such as in snail shells. It also relates to the "golden rectangle", where the length and breadth of the shape are Fibonacci numbers.

The recognition of the presence of this number in nature is by no means new. However, this beautiful sequence only started becoming more widely known as the Fibonacci sequence after Leonardo of Pisa explored and systematically described it in 1202. It was first discovered in India about 13,000 years ago. It has featured in art and philosophy in many different forms in many different places.

Many artists across the ages have celebrated the divinity of these numerals in their work. To them, the golden ratio is the ultimate expression of beauty. Matthew Cross spent thirty minutes in his TED talk to demonstrate how new understanding is gained by changing the way we represent things. He makes it apparent that numbers are expressed in many different forms in the natural world and that simply by symbolizing this number in different ways, we even create beauty through art and music.

Galileo famously said that "the language of the universe is mathematics". Hopefully, you now have a greater understanding of why he said this. This vision of numbers as the most fundamental conceptual component of the fabric of the universe is central to numerology. We must adopt a fresh vocabulary from which we can come to understand ourselves in new ways by using numerology.

On that note, let us proceed in learning more about Pythagorean numerology in a historical context so that you can begin your journey to establishing your numerology chart.

Chapter 3: The History of Numerology

https://www.pexels.com/photo/photography-of-opened-book-1172018/

In a vast number of history books, Pythagoras was given credit for being the founder of modern numerology. While his theories are popularly used today, the general consensus is that states such as India, Babylon, Japan, and Egypt were using number systems long before Pythagoras organized them in the systematic way that he did. If we were to take a step back in time to the ancient world that existed before

NUMEROLOGY MADE EASY

Pythagoras, no matter which culture we visit, we would be almost guaranteed to find some form of astrology or numerology. It was part-and-parcel of the deep connection that people had with each other and with the natural world.

Although numerology can be traced back to ancient times, it was only in 1907 that its term was coined by Dr. Julian Stenton. Ten years later, the first book on numerology was published by L. Dow Balliett. It was entitled *The Philosophy of Numbers: Their Tone and Color.*

However, modern-day numerological methods and interpretations vary slightly from one culture to another based on cultural and philosophical differences, as well as the nature of the consciousness of each community (Ducie 2015). The most prominent systems that we have inherited from the ancient world include the Kabbalah, Chaldean, and Pythagorean systems. Pythagorean numerology is the most popular and accurate form of the field used today, and it is the system that will be adopted in this book.

In this chapter, we will learn more about the history of these different systems and focus on Pythagoras, his numbering system, and what makes the Pythagorean method unique.

NUMEROLOGY MADE EASY

Pythagorean Numerology

https://www.pexels.com/photo/woman-writing-on-a-whiteboard-3862130/

In the previous chapter, when you envisioned your dreaded mathematics class, you may have seen triangles and Greek letters on the board in front of you. Your syllabus probably, for a brief interlude at least, featured the works of Pythagoras. Pythagorean numerology is based on his views of the harmony of numbers as the fundamental basis upon which reality bursts into manifestation from infinite potential.

NUMEROLOGY MADE EASY

Whether we like him or not, the incorrigible Pythagoras has not only sneaked into our math textbooks, but on a more profound level, also into the heart of the understanding of all numbers that we have inherited from centuries-worth of study. What he communicated through his work was a universal understanding of the profound way in which numbers form the fabric of our realities, as has been described in previous chapters.

Pythagoras was a mystic, mathematician, and philosopher who was alive during a time in ancient Greece when psychology was still seen as relating to the soul more than the mind. The story goes that Pythagoras was walking past a blacksmith one day and noticed how the notes he heard sounded curiously harmonious. Upon deeper exploration of this observation, he realized that the anvils were in whole-number ratios to one another. Thus, he established a connection between whole numbers and harmony.

However, there is more to his belief system than what is described in this story. Pythagoras believed that numbers are the essence of the whole universe. He was known for commonly using the expression "all things are numbers". As such, he believed that numbers can be used to understand the world, especially the numbers one through four, which form the building blocks of all other numbers. Pythagoras believed that numerals are the subtle, largely-unseen potential from which physical reality manifests itself. (Numerology Secrets, 2015).

So far in this section, we have looked briefly at the life of Pythagoras, as well as the ins and outs of the complex body of knowledge that he lived, breathed, and shared with many great thinkers who appeared in his wake, such as Plato, Socrates, and St. Augustine. Many of his ideas have stood the test of time, enduring the tides of change. The world today looks much different from the world in which Pythagoras made his mark. However, the eternal truths of his theories have as much relevance today as they did back then, when the world was a much smaller place (Numerology Explained, 2020).

Pythagorean, Kabbalah, and Chaldean Numerology

The idea in numerology is that the circumstances into which you were born play a pivotal role in determining various conditions in your life, such as

NUMEROLOGY MADE EASY

your personality, destiny, and life circumstances, to name a few. In Pythagorean numerology, particularly, your birth name and birthdate are two important determining features in who you are and in how your life plays out. Your birthdate and the letters of your name carry an energetic imprint that can be used to help you navigate your future. Secondly, this particular system is based on the numbers one through nine.

As well as being one of the most accurate systems available to us, the Pythagorean approach uses the English alphabet that we know of and love. It has already been suggested that Pythagoras was churning out his theories long after other cultures, such as those in India and China already established a number system.

Rewinding a few thousand years and zooming in on ancient Babylon will reveal another culture that used numbers for divinatory and mystical purposes. The Chaldean numerology system is the oldest known system. In contrast to Pythagorean numerology, Chaldean numerology does not correlate numbers with letters in alphabetical order. Rather, numerals are organized according to the resonance of each letter. For the people of ancient Mesopotamia, sound and inflections played an integral role in divination.

NUMEROLOGY MADE EASY

Yes, numbers have their place in the web of life, but also in the leagues of the supernatural. Another difference between this method and the Pythagorean one is that the Chaldeans use a "one to eight" numbering system. This is because the number nine was considered sacred and treated differently from the preceding numbers.

Most numerological systems consist of numerals one through nine, as these make up all other more complex numbers. Some frameworks also include zero and/or ten for specific reasons that are beyond the scope of this book.

Chapter 4: The Basics of Numerology

https://www.pexels.com/photo/abc-books-chalk-chalkboard-265076/

Up to this point, we have dived into the past to shine a light on the birthplace of numerology. We have also discovered what numerology is.

In this chapter, we will learn about the basic principles and methods regarding what modern numerology entails. This will enable you to proceed with working out your numbers in the forthcoming chapters. We will also touch on some hints and tips that you may find useful in developing your numerology chart.

Getting started may seem daunting at this point. You may be overwhelmed by the prospect of doing mathematical equations, especially after reading the complex theories described above. However, the sums involved in numerology are quite basic and only require you to add numbers together. Once you know the basic method, you will find that it is quite simple; you will get the hang of it in no time!

There are **two methods that can be used to work out your numbers**. Some of the differences between certain Numerological theories were discussed earlier. The system that is used in this book is inherited from the Pythagorean method and ascribes value to letters of the name, as well as numbers. Unlike the Chaldean method, it uses the zero-to-nine numbering system rather than the zero-to-eight.

The correlation chart is included in this chapter for reference; you will need to refer to it later to figure out your individual numbers. It was mentioned earlier that different systems also have various number systems upon which their method is based. The one

NUMEROLOGY MADE EASY

that will be used in this book is based on the zero-to-nine model:

1	2	3	4	5	6	7	8	9
A	B	C	D	E	F	G	H	I
J	K	L	M	N	O	P	Q	R
S	T	U	V	W	X	Y	Z	

When you reduce your number down to a single digit, there are two scenarios in which you will retain the double digit as well as the final single digit. Firstly, the numbers 11, 22, and 33 are regarded as "master numbers". They are of a higher octave than single digits and thus resonate at a higher frequency.

The second situation in which you will keep your double digit is if it is one of the following numbers: 13, 14, 16, or 19. These four numbers are considered numerals for "karmic debt" and are written as 13/4, 14/5, 16/7, and 19/1, respectively.

Master numbers and karmic debt will be dealt with in later chapters, but for now, keep them in mind when you are working out your core numbers.

Chapter 5: The Meaning of Numbers

https://www.pexels.com/photo/scientific-calculator-ii-5775/

The idea behind karma and numerology, and one that is adopted by those who subscribe to these belief systems, is that you enter into this particular lifetime with a specific intention. Numbers can help you bring this into your consciousness so that you can achieve what you originally set out to. You can identify challenges and themes that are communicated to you

NUMEROLOGY MADE EASY

through the patterns and cycles of numbers in your life.

While this book will give you a set of interpretations of the numbers one through nine, it should be emphasized that they are not intended to be applied as hard-and-fast gospel truth. The emphasis here is to use the interpretations of the numbers that are offered as a guide.

Similarly, you might even find that the Pythagorean numerology system does not resonate with you as much as another one does. What is required is for you to be honest with yourself about what strikes a chord with you and what does not. What is most important is that you ultimately find your own truth. Hopefully, whether you pursue Pythagorean numerology or not, this book will empower you with the knowledge to enable you to continue your journey one way or another.

Numerology requires us not only to be flexible about what information is received from a guide such as this, but also to let go of attachment to particular meanings in specific moments when we are aware of a particular number pattern.

NUMEROLOGY MADE EASY

Nature is a good teacher if we pay attention to her, and the number one option is to be able to let go of any preconceptions or biases we have. We must do so in order to open space for whatever teachings we receive intuitively. At the end of the day, a numerological interpretation is a very personal and intimate process that only you can be responsible for.

When it comes to interpreting the numbers in your life, there can be many possibilities. Michele Buchanan highlights the importance of using common sense when applying the opinion of others to analyze the significant numbers in your life. It goes without saying that you should consider which suggestions are applicable to you and which are not. However, it is important that you are honest with yourself during this process.

In cases where you don't recognize a quality in yourself that is described by your number, Buchanan emphasizes the importance of being aware of opportunities to embody that quality at a later point in your life, even if you don't see it as part of who you are at present.

It is a common mistake for people new to numerology to judge the strengths, qualities, and challenges that are presented in a numerology reading.

NUMEROLOGY MADE EASY

In modern society, there are noticeable trends regarding what is considered beautiful or admirable in a person. These kinds of stereotypes can relate to race, gender, and occupation, to name a few.

They cut deep into our psyches and play a large role in determining how we judge others and ourselves on a personal level. Numbers do not discriminate, and neither should you. This ancient system of understanding the world should be used as a practical guide for creating the life you love.

It is important that you take time to work through at least the main core numbers, which Buchanan calls the "personality numbers", before reaching any conclusions or making vital decisions. Any reading should be done with a holistic view in mind. Only once you have worked out all your numbers and explored their possible meanings will you get a clearer picture. You should also give yourself time to process what you learn.

In this chapter, we will explore what the numbers one through nine might mean for the personality numbers that will be calculated in this book. The perspective provided here is based on the one offered by Michele Buchanan in her book *Numerology*.

NUMEROLOGY MADE EASY

NUMEROLOGY MADE EASY

The Meaning of the Numbers 1 - 9

Each number listed here has both positive and negative qualities. Nobody is perfect, and we all have our doubts, secret shadows and pasts. These numbers help us to recognize our strengths so that we can live them out to their full potential. They also realize our weaknesses so that we may recognize, acknowledge, and improve upon them. Everyone can work out what numbers they are by referencing the numerology chart and solving their numbers by the letters in their names.

Number one: Number ones are known for their strong will and independence. They are not afraid to stand out from the crowd, especially if it means being able to express their creative potential to its full capacity. The fire of motivation with ones burns from within. When they tap into their self-authority, they are able to overcome the need for approval from others.

Given these characteristics, it should come as no surprise that, in terms of career, number ones often choose occupations that allow them the freedom to manage their own time, such as managing their own businesses. If they do have a job, they function best in a leadership or management position. They find it easy to cut through obstacles they may face in the achievement of their goals.

If left unattended, these qualities can make the number one quite aggressive and controlling. They can be overly competitive, intolerant, and impatient. One of the focus areas for this person is to better understand their relationship with others and develop a higher degree of self-awareness.

Number two: Number twos are natural-born peacemakers and healers who would prefer to avoid conflict, even if it means personal sacrifice. They are generally likable by most but are very sensitive to their environments, energy, and other people. Thus, the management of their own space is important for them.

In the light, their sensitivity manifests as a gift for intuition, which makes them excellent at being able to empathize with others. Twos often take on the role of the counselor with friends and family, if they don't take on that position professionally. In the dark, this can make them prone to hypersensitivity and moodiness.

NUMEROLOGY MADE EASY

Twos work well in a loving partnership but can be insecure and jealous if they feel threatened. They can also succumb to indecision.

Number three: The qualities of a person who has a number three personality are hard to miss, as they love being the center of attention. Threes are colorful, creative, and artistic people who are charismatic and often entertaining.

They are in their element when able to express themselves, and their gifts may be expressed in different ways. Some find expression better through words, while others find more sense of satisfaction by expressing themselves artistically. Threes often have a good sense of humor and are usually the life of the party.

The shadow aspects of a three come out largely in the mismanagement of their self-expression. They can use their capacity for expression in harmful or co-dependent ways through gossip or by being judgmental or overly critical. They can be demanding and attention-seeking if they do not get the spotlight they desire; they can also be melodramatic. Threes can be hard to keep up with as their energy easily becomes scattered.

NUMEROLOGY MADE EASY

Number four: You can count on a number four to get the job done. Practical, grounded, and reliable, people with a number four personality are hard workers who know the meaning of integrity and perseverance. They focus on accuracy and attention to detail, and their strengths also lie in being organized and responsible.

They tend to keep their thoughts and emotions to themselves and need stability in their physical and emotional affairs in order to conquer. However, their tendency to be highly practical can result in rigidity and intolerance. They can also be close-minded, stubborn, and pessimistic.

Number five: People who have this number as one of their personality numbers tend to be adaptable and relish variety and change. They are often good at a number of things; you might find them building furniture one week and brewing beer the next. Their capacity to be a jack-of-all-trades can take form in their working life as well, and you might find that they change jobs regularly. This can be, in part, due to the resistance they often have to making commitments, which can also affect the nature of their relationships.

Number fives can easily fall victim to the physical pleasures of substances, food, and sex. Fives can be social butterflies and have a natural affinity for communication and lifting others up. In this sense, they can be quite charismatic. Like the number threes, number fives can sometimes be a little unfocused, melodramatic, and erratic.

Number six: The priority for number sixes is relationships. Naturally generous and caring, a number six is always willing to help someone in need. They are loyal, caring, and happy to be of service one way or another in whatever way possible. The downside to their giving natures is that they are easily manipulated and taken advantage of. They also struggle to balance self-care with helping others, often at their own expense.

They are constantly learning about boundaries, especially between helping others and interfering. They struggle to find a balance between giving and receiving and often have difficulty with the latter.

Number sixes are frequently motivated, often to unhealthy levels, by their need to achieve and sometimes have difficulty knowing when to draw the line. They have a scarcity mentality about how much they are giving and are constantly doubting that they are doing enough. They struggle to recognize their own, and other peoples', darkness.

NUMEROLOGY MADE EASY

Number seven: Number sevens embody truth-seeking qualities. They have a natural thirst for knowledge and understanding and an affinity for learning. The content they are interested in varies from person to person, but no matter what they are called to inquire into, they find meaning in seeking answers.

Number sevens value time to themselves for introspection, and this is vital for them to remain grounded in a chaotic world. Sevens, in particular, enjoy spending time in nature and benefit from activities like meditation or yoga. Their journey is to find the truth from within, rather than looking to external sources for answers.

The strengths here are being analytically-minded, having an affinity for the technical aspects of things, and being highly intellectual. Being prone to live in their mental worlds, number sevens can be pessimistic, cynical, and suspicious. They themselves can be quite closed-hearted, cold, and secretive.

Number eight: The emphasis with number eight personalities is that the power of the mind plays an irrevocable role in determining their realities. Being motivated and having the willingness to put in the hard work to achieve their goals, number eights have the potential to create a life of abundance for themselves. In these cases, it is possible for the eight to be too controlling, and people can easily be intimidated by them because of this. Or, it could go the other way.

A number eight might experience great scarcity in their lives because of their beliefs, and this may persist until they learn to overcome their self-sabotaging ways via methods that are not manipulative. Eights do particularly well when they can be their own bosses or when they take leadership roles in their working environments.

Number nine: Number nines are generally empathetic, generous, and moved by problems in the world to help others or contribute to rectifying problems in the natural world. They also express their compassion with the people they are close to, taking pleasure in giving them gifts.

They have a deep-seated sense of compassion that, when combined with their potentially fiery and passionate nature, makes them formidable in the fight for any cause. This red-hot passion can make them relentless in their pursuit of justice, bordering on aggressive as they fail sometimes to recognize the need for diplomacy and balance.

They are broad-minded and usually have a diverse range of experiences that help teach them to be less judgmental. They can be quite defensive when taken to task.

NUMEROLOGY MADE EASY

Master Numbers

https://www.pexels.com/photo/silhouette-of-man-at-daytime-1051838/

As mentioned before, master numbers are when any of your personality numbers come to a total of 11, 22, or 33. These numerals reflect a higher frequency version of your single-digit number, and the choice is always yours about which path you will take. According to Buchanan, people who have master numbers have a number of general characteristics that set them apart from others who don't, though some choose not to embody their higher potential in this lifetime.

NUMEROLOGY MADE EASY

For one reason, some people with master numbers have a higher frequency than others and a strong desire to make a difference in the world. However, in order to embody the potential of the master number, they often face many challenges and obstacles, and their lives may seem complex.

Manifesting the qualities of the master number requires resilience to overcome the challenges of the single-digit numbers, and this often happens only after the age of 45.

After this age, they are more able to practice groundedness, confidence, and balance. Before they are able to do this, they may succumb to sensitivity, anxiety, and self-doubt before they are fully able to allow their intuitive and psychic gifts to come to fruition.

You now have a general idea of the basic strengths and weaknesses of people with master numbers. Of course, these are not set in stone and depend on the nature and history of the person in question. Below are more specific details about each of the master numbers. Each one includes the characteristics of the core numbers and has additional qualities.

NUMEROLOGY MADE EASY

Number 11/2: Through their own journey of transformation, people with master number eleven can teach others through their own experience. Number elevens are highly sensitive and intuitive people. Before this can manifest as the inspirational qualities of the teacher, the number eleven must learn to use the nervous, scattered energy of the two for the higher good without being overwhelmed by anxiety.

Other challenges faced by people with this master number are overcoming their natural capacity for manipulation and insecurity. They are also prone to be delusional and overly intense. Through learning more about themselves and overcoming their inner demons, number elevens can transmute their own desires and harmonize them with the greater good with a broader perspective.

Number 22/4: People with master number twenty-two have the same characteristics as people who have four as their core number with the potential to excel at bringing potential or vision into concrete reality. They can improve upon structures that exist in physical reality, such as businesses or organizations. Like the beaver, number twenty-twos are master builders and can transform basic building blocks into their highest potential on the physical plane.

NUMEROLOGY MADE EASY

However, first, they must recognize the need for inter-dependence in co-creating and let go of their insecurities, doubts, and fears and take the plunge that will enable their great success. Before they become the builder, they must recognize their proclivity for stubbornness, inflexibility, and a tendency to control others, as well as harness their tendency to overwork themselves in pursuit of their goals. The mind of the twenty-two is often up in the sky. This idealistic, visionary quality can be of vital importance in bridging the spiritual and physical worlds for themselves, for others, and for the greater good.

Number 33/6: So far, the master numbers have revealed the inner teacher and builder in those who have chosen the path of the master. Number thirty-three sheds light on the potential of the healer. What many who have this number don't realize is that healing can have a variety of forms, including the more conventional medical form of healing and alternative healing methods, as well as the creative arts, for example.

There is immense potential in sound, comedy, mythology, and the art of healing, as well. Like the previous master numbers, people with thirty-three have the same attributes and challenges as those with six as a core number. However, threes have great creative potential and need to learn to do this productively.

The gifts of the 33/6 lie in their compassionate, nurturing natures as well as their bottomless well of creativity, while their challenges include being overly self-critical and self-righteous over-achievers. On another note, some numerologists don't consider thirty-three as a master number, believing that only eleven and twenty-two are master numbers.

Chapter 6: The Personality Numbers

We have already acknowledged that the people of the ancient world and numerologists working today differ in their approaches. While the cross-cultural exchange of knowledge and ideas may have changed the way global reality evolved, today, our access to information from even the most obscure places has reached unimaginable levels. Knowledge over the centuries has died and been reborn countless times, and soon it will begin to take on new characteristics. In this way, it almost represents the cosmic cycle of death and rebirth.

The point is that different numerologists have different preferences about what to include in their readings. This being said, there are a few numbers that are used universally that create a solid foundation upon which you can build your empire of numerological knowledge. These are the life path number, the personality number, the soul number, the birthday number, and the destiny number.

NUMEROLOGY MADE EASY

The purpose of this book is not to lay out the technical details of this art, but rather to provide you with a basic infrastructure upon which you can create a better understanding. It also seeks to give you a taste of how to interpret numbers in your life and to gain a greater sense of self-trust in recognizing which systems resonate with you. Along the way, one or two different perspectives will be provided that will enable you to compare different styles, in addition to providing you with a few sets of perspectives from which you can choose your ideal approach.

So, in the next few chapters, we will explore how to work out some of the main numbers that are used by most numerologists. These terms are often referred to by different names. As we explore each of these important numbers, we will also look at the various names by which they are known.

Michele Buchanan adds two more to the list: The current name number and the maturity number. However, we will focus on the first four in this book as they form the backbone of most approaches. You can then use the information of the numbers one through nine described in the chapter entitled "The Meaning of Numbers" to interpret each of these. This way, you will be able to form a picture of your soul's journey through this lifetime.

NUMEROLOGY MADE EASY

Each of the personality numbers mentioned in this book has a light and dark side to their energies. They have the potential to bring out both your strengths and weaknesses, and you may recognize some of both in yourself. We would like to reiterate that you should try your very best to eliminate any sense of judgment that you have toward yourself when creating your chart. Numerology simply offers you another perspective; it is your choice to take it or leave it. The positives that are highlighted for each number simply emphasize the potential you have for that quality, whether you have embodied it yet or not.

By recognizing your shadow, or your weaknesses, you can live with greater fullness of being. It is too easy for us to subscribe to the pursuit of perfection and compromise our happiness in pursuit of trying to be flawless. This is a modern concept that amounts to love that is conditional. When you approach the teachings that numbers have to offer, doing so with an open heart and mind can help you to find a greater degree of self acceptance.

We have all heard this expression in one form or another: "You need the dark in order to appreciate the light", or, "You can't know joy if you haven't experienced suffering". In order to step into our fullest potential, we need to accept the parts of ourselves we don't like. In many spiritual practices, self-acceptance is an inevitable part of the process.

In mindfulness practice, for example, life is simply not complete without darkness. Life as we know it could not exist without the cycles of day and night. In this same way, we are able to walk through life with a lighter step if we love ourselves for who we are.

The Life Path Number

https://www.pexels.com/photo/photo-of-pathway-surrounded-by-fir-trees-1578750/

NUMEROLOGY MADE EASY

The life path number is probably one of the most well-known concepts in numerology and other spiritual approaches. You may have heard the life path being referred to in palmistry or other arts. It is one of the most important tools in divination, because it helps to paint a picture of our purpose in life that transcends our own egotistical desires and conceptions of what we want to achieve. In this sense, it provides a broader perspective of who we are destined to be based on the date of our birth, and it may give an idea of the challenges that we might face along the way to fulfilling our greater purpose. It focuses on the light that is within us, rather than projecting darkness into our future (Ducie 2015).

In contrast to some of the other numbers, the life path number helps to give us a general sense of who we are and what we have intended to do with our lives on a deeper level (Earl Anderson, 2018). This is based on a broader picture yourself in the context of the universe as a whole - and in the context of your previous lifetimes.

It refers to the purpose of your life in a more profound sense than simply referring to your career or job. It provides you with a holistic picture of the experiences you might have in this lifetime, who you truly are as a person, and the lessons you are here to learn. In a practical sense, being aware of our life path number can help us align our inner and outer realities (Ducie 2015), bringing our soul's purpose to fruition on the physical plane.

If you have done further research about numerology, you may have noticed that the life path number is sometimes referred to as the "soul aspiration number", the "life purpose number", or the "fate number" (Ducie, 2015). It is also commonly called the "ruling number", "birth path", "birth force number", and, in Chaldean numerology, it is referred to as the "destiny number" (Numerology Explained, 2020).

The life path number is worked out by adding up all the numbers in your full date of birth. As mentioned earlier, there are three ways for figuring this out, but we will use the reducing-down method.

Let's use the birthdate September 27th, 1963 as an example:

Step 1: Add up the digits in the day, month, and year respectively, thereby reducing them down to a single digit.

2 + 7	9	1 + 9 + 6 + 3 = 19
= **9**	**9**	1 + 9 = 10
		1 + 0 = **1**

Step 2: Keep adding and reducing, until you get a single-digit number.

9 + 9 + 1 = 19

1 + 9 = 10

1 + 0 = **1**

Here you can see that the life path number is one.

The Destiny Number

The destiny number is more specific than the life path number and helps reveal our personal gifts, skills, talents, and characteristics. Ducie (2015) believed that this "overall self-expression number" contains all of the wisdom about your soul's journey. You may notice that it can refer to gifts that you have used in the past.

NUMEROLOGY MADE EASY

This number is more popularly referred to as the "expression number", but it is sometimes called the "name number". In terms of helping you on a practical level, it can help guide you in making decisions about your relationships and career. This number highlights our individual strengths and weaknesses so that we can come to know ourselves better. It enables us to make a conscious choice about the degree to which we let our shadow traits govern our lives, as well as focus our attention on developing our talents and gifts for the benefit of ourselves and others.

To work out your destiny number, you need to add up the numerical values of each letter of your full birth name, whether or not you still use that name today. That is, you should use the name that is on your birth certificate, but without including titles or suffixes. For example, when you are calculating this number, you should not use "Miss", "Mrs", "Mr", "Dr", "Jr", or "Snr".

Note that the name on your birth certificate still applies if you have changed your name through marriage or the use of your adopted name. Your destiny number can't be changed; it reflects the conditions of this lifetime that you birthed yourself

NUMEROLOGY MADE EASY

into, and it is a microcosmic representation of the harmony of the universe.

Step one: Work out the number that correlates with each letter of your birth name using the table:

1	2	3	4	5	6	7	8	9
A	B	C	D	E	F	G	H	I
J	K	L	M	N	O	P	Q	R
S	T	U	V	W	X	Y	Z	

Let's use Sam Joe Smith as an example:

S	A	M		J	O	E		S	M	I	T	H
1	1	4		1	6	5		1	4	9	2	8

Step two: Add them all together. As before, keep adding them until you have a single digit number.

1 + 1 + 4   1 + 6 + 5   1 + 4 + 9 + 2 + 8

2 + 4 = **6**   1 + 2 = **3**   2 + 4 = **6**

6 + 3 + 6 = **15**

1 + 5 = **6**

6 is the destiny number for Sam Joe Smith.

NUMEROLOGY MADE EASY

The Soul Number

If you explore other sources on the topic of numerology, you will find that the soul number is also sometimes referred to as your "heart's desire", "soul's desire", or "soul's urge". This is because it relates to who you need to be or what sort of life you need to live in order for your soul to have a sense of completion.

Earl Anderson (2018) calls this the "heart's desire" number. It delves into the inner clockwork of the heart and inner self, exploring your deep-seated motivations and dreams.

The soul number is calculated by adding up the numeric value of each of the vowels in your birth name. Note that you can use "Y" as a vowel if there are no other vowels in the syllable or if three is a consonant on both sides of it.

Let's use Sam Joe Smith as an example name:

NUMEROLOGY MADE EASY

1	2	3	4	5	6	7	8	9
A	B	C	D	E	F	G	H	I
J	K	L	M	N	O	P	Q	R
S	T	U	V	W	X	Y	Z	

S **A** M   J **O** **E** S M **I** T H
    1   6   5   9

1 + 6 + 5 + 9 = 21

2 + 1 = 3

The soul number for Sam Joe Smith is three.

The Personality Number

The personality number is considered the least important of the numbers. It provides information about how others see you - the personality that you project into the world and that you allow to be seen by others (although you may not be conscious of it) (Buchanan, 2015).

It draws our attention to the psychological and emotional patterns that we started developing when we were children and the way that we were conditioned. By exploring the personality number, we allow ourselves to welcome the possibility of being able to let go of those patterns (Ducie 2015).

From *Numerology Explained (2015)*, it is the side of yourself that you show to the world. It doesn't show every element of your personality, just the side of yourself that you show to the world. This number can provide a reflection about the kinds of first impressions you tend to make on other people, and how others might see you.

The personality number is calculated by adding up the consonants of your name.

The Birthday Number

The birthday number is simply the day on which you were born. It is sometimes called the "day born number" or the "day number". If it is a double digit, reduce it down to a single digit to get your birthday number.

It is believed that the day of your birth can be used to help you gain a better understanding of the specific skills you have been incarnated with in this lifetime.

NUMEROLOGY MADE EASY

This can help you fulfill your true purpose as well as embody your potential. Using these natural gifts can assist you on your own journey, and it can also be of great value to others in this world (Numerology Explained, 2020).

Chapter 7: Karma and Karmic Debt

Put simply, karma is the universal law of cause and effect. Essentially, what you put out comes back to you. There is truth in the statement "what goes around comes around". Karma can occur on a personal level, but also on the level of the collective.

Millions of people across the world and from different cultures believe in the idea of karma. Some people believe that it is functional in helping you to reach the end of a cycle, or, to state it another way, to become enlightened. Others think that karma and reincarnation are part of an endless cycle that will continue to repeat indefinitely.

The good news is that we can do something about karma. We can set the intention to allow the negative patterns in our lives to end. This is not to say that simply by being more positive, nothing bad will ever happen to you.

However, setting an intention can at least help you become more aware of the challenges that arise and to slip through them more effortlessly. Numerology is a framework or worldview that can help you identify unresolved issues.

Karmic Lessons

There are two karma-related principles in numerology: Karmic lessons and karmic debt. We will begin exploring these concepts by looking at karmic lesson numbers first, later focusing on karmic debt.

Your karmic lesson number relates to unresolved weaknesses or challenges that have accompanied you in this incarnation because you failed to resolve them in previous lifetimes. Not everyone has a karmic lesson number, though. Some people have a karmic lesson number and learn the lesson fairly quickly. On the other hand, others are more resistant to learning the lesson described by their numbers. For these people, karmic energy can build up over time and sudden, dramatic change takes place.

Note that when you are doing your reading, if the number is the same as your life path, destiny,

NUMEROLOGY MADE EASY

birthday, or personality number, its influence is minimized.

The karmic lesson number is established by looking at which numbers you don't have in the name on your birth certificate. It, therefore, makes sense that another name that these numbers are known by is "missing numbers". This is referring to the numbers that are absent from your full name.

Number one: If your karmic lesson number is one, your lesson relates to establishing more independence in this life, having the courage to go against the tide and not be so reliant upon others to provide for you.

Number two: The number two as a karmic lesson number brings to light the need for you to recognize others in your life, to empathize with them and be more generous toward them. It also emphasizes the need to learn to work with others in achieving your goals.

Number three: This number reveals the importance of learning to embrace your talents to their fullest potential. If you heed the direction given to you given by this number, you will learn to become less rigid and critical in your views of life and yourself.

Number four: If you have four as your karmic lesson number, the emphasis is placed on adopting a more responsible role in your life. This may require you to learn how to manage your life better through improved organizational skills. Number fours will also learn the necessity of hard work in achieving their goals.

Number five: Karmic lesson five reveals the need to learn about flexibility and develop the ability to adapt to changing circumstances. This may highlight the need to take a more open and outgoing attitude toward life.

Number six: Having the karmic lesson number six means that you will need to realize the importance of forging meaningful relationships with others. It also emphasizes the need to take more responsibility in your life.

Number seven: This number will teach you that you need to see beyond the veil of illusion in the material world and gain a deeper faith in spiritual matters. You might need to learn to open your heart more to other people in order to see this.

NUMEROLOGY MADE EASY

Number eight: If eight is your karmic lesson number, the lesson for you in this life is to reclaim your power in the physical realm.

Number nine: Number nine as a karmic lesson number teaches you about the importance of forgiveness. If this is your number, you still need to learn about unconditional acceptance and being less critical of others

Karmic Debt

NUMEROLOGY MADE EASY

https://www.pexels.com/photo/american-dollar-banknote-on-table-4386153/

Karmic debt refers to the important lessons that you still have to learn. People who subscribe to the idea of reincarnation believe that this is based on the experiences in previous lifetimes.

If you don't pay attention to the karmic themes that appear in your life, they will continue to repeat themselves until you learn the lesson. Identifying your karmic debt number helps to bring it to the surface of your subconscious so that you can be more aware of it when it is happening.

There are four karmic debt numbers that people should be aware of. These are 13, 14, 16, and 19.

Karmic debt number 13/4: The emphasis with this karmic debt number is hard work and effort. You need to realize through your experience that the greatest gains are made by perseverance and effort rather than choosing the path of least resistance. This may be related to experiences in your last life where you allowed others to do the work for you.

Karmic debt number 14/5: The primary lesson to be learned by people who have fourteen as a karmic debt number is moderation. As we learned in the previous chapter, if you have this as one of your personality numbers, you may be prone to overindulgence and excess. To overcome this, you need to practice moderation, balance, and self-control. That is, you should allow yourself to enjoy your life without compromising your commitments and sacrificing fulfilling your promises.

Karmic debt number 16/7: What is required here is for you to peel through the layers of superficiality that you tend to create that smother what is really important to you. You need to be able to put your ego aside and see yourself as part of a wider community and greater reality. Allow the process of the universe to unfold; this will help you to navigate the unexpected events that are out of control in your life.

Pay attention to reflecting on your core values, and re-evaluate them so that they are in better alignment with your higher self.

Karmic debt number 19/1: With an unresolved karmic debt number of 19/1, you experience frustration when you realize you aren't able to control people to the extent that you would like to. To release the energy of this karmic debt, you need to develop a greater sense of empathy and consideration for other people. You may also be required to drop into a sense of humility to recognize when you are wrong and accept the help of others when needed. To be able to walk in the shoes of others, it is required for you to move through this debt.

Up to this point in the book, you have increased your knowledge regarding what numerology is, and you have learned about how to draw up your own numerology chart including five of the central numbers used in Pythagorean numerology. We have seen how, within this framework, your past lives influence who you are in this lifetime.

It is beyond the scope of this book to go into detail about all the possible numbers you can have in your chart, so the next chapter will describe what else you might expect from a reading if you were to see a professional numerologist, or if you were to explore the subject in greater depth on your own.

Chapter 8: Other Numbers in Your Numerology Chart

The Current Name Number

Up to now, you have learned how to work out some of the most commonly used numbers that can help you draw up a numerological chart of your own. However, numbers can help us in more ways than just providing an one-off overall compass; they can also give us a road map when dealing with specific questions we ask ourselves on a day-to-day basis.

In addition to the primary numbers mentioned above, numerology also offers a forecast for the future through various "forecasting numbers". These include the personal year, month, and day numbers, as well as universal numbers, which describe the global annual, monthly, and daily cycles. One of the ways in which numbers can help guide us in our everyday life is through our personal year number.

NUMEROLOGY MADE EASY

Once you start noticing numbers, you may find that recurring numerals start showing up. They can be any number and appear in any context imaginable, such as cell phone numbers, license plates, addresses, or the time. Recurring numbers can have meanings ascribed to the individual digits, but keep in mind that your interpretation of them may vary from one context to another.

When we are faced with decisions, many of us are crippled by paralysis that is induced by the mind. By adopting the view that numbers can guide us through our lives, we can simplify our decision-making process. Once we start recognizing the numeric cycles that happen in our lives, we can use them to give meaning to the experiences we have and make decisions that are more in harmony with natural laws rather than wading through the muddy waters of our minds.

Many of us have been in situations where we were unable to make decisions. This is because we get lost in the territory of our tyrannical minds that are so easily influenced by forces in the external world. With numerology, we can take control of how we make decisions and do so harmoniously with nature. As with many of the other esoteric arts, in numerology, choices should be made with the heart rather than the head.

The kinds of decisions that numerology can help us with include gaining a deeper understanding of our health and making more conscious choices relating to it, as well as making decisions with regards to our career, creating healthier relationships, and even choosing life partners.

Solving Your Number for Your Career

NUMEROLOGY MADE EASY

https://www.pexels.com/photo/adult-business-computer-contemporary-380769/

Life path numbers are very significant to people who want to use numerology to help guide their lives and their choices. These different types of choices can vary from great to small, because basing them on significant numbers can help you make the best types of choices. Solving your personal number for your career is greatly needed if you want to be fully successful in what you choose to do.

If you are currently feeling dissatisfied or unsure of the type of career path that you have chosen, then you may be following the wrong one. This doesn't mean that you won't be successful in what you are doing now, but you may not be entirely satisfied. You could be unconsciously drawn to particular types of careers because you are predisposed to enjoy that line of work. Numerology works like that.

When you are trying to solve your career number, then you should try your best to allow the advice and guidance from numerology to aid you along your way. Understanding that different life path numbers will direct you towards different career paths will allow you to choose the right career path for your life. Many of these are generalized and will include several "similar" careers together. This means that you may notice your desired career path falls inside the spectrum of careers that you should follow.

Number ones should follow a path that allows them to be leaders. Because ones are generally more authoritative and can be stronger than others, they will automatically be inclined to lead others. Ones can find it difficult to compromise in many situations. They normally keep the mentality "it's my way or the highway", and they don't let people forget it. This type of mentality, however, does make it more likely that others will go to them for guidance, because many people are drawn to strong leaders.

Because ones are so inclined to lead, they normally thrive as entrepreneurs or businessmen. Ones do function well with others around them, but it can cause conflict if there are a few ones in a single room. Some ones get irritated with this type of conflict because it wastes time, so they are prone to work on their own or specifically choose who works with them.

Number twos are more caring types of people. They are able to look at different perspectives and make unbiased decisions based on the facts that are presented to them. Twos generally are attracted to career paths that are more socially inclined since they like to help others. Twos are often the most diplomatic types of people, and because of this, they thrive in careers that need unbiased opinions.

Twos are best suited in career paths that are centered around diplomacy. Medical doctors, lawyers, teachers, psychologists, counselors, politicians, and religious ministers are often twos. There are, of course, exceptions, but generally speaking, twos are the best suited for these types of roles.

Number threes are very creative people. This means that they should pursue a career that is more creativity-based. Threes are normally very energetic and love being around people. Threes love to be social but they do tend to enjoy being the center of attention, which means they can be prone to talking instead of listening.

Threes love to entertain others, which means that they tend to move into careers of comedians, actors, or even travel journalists. Because of the creative nature of threes, they should pursue a career that allows them to embrace their creative side instead of suppressing it.

Number fours have excellent organizational skills. This means that they are logical, sensible, and rather well-disciplined in their everyday activities. Number fours tend to move away from everyday social activities as they tend to prefer their own company. Many fours follow career paths that require individual work and a lot of self-discipline.

They are very well-suited to follow paths that include numbers, such as accountants, financial planners, lab technicians, engineers, and project managers. Any job that requires a person in need of a lot of self-discipline would appeal to a four.

Number fives are excellent at communication and can even be rather persuasive at times. They tend to develop a passion for adventurous undertakings (and daydream about those adventures if they are stuck in nine-to-five jobs).

Fives are drawn to careers that don't necessarily limit them to sitting behind a desk. This opens up possible careers in public relations, radio, advertising, and travel journalism.

Number sixes are generally known as peacekeepers. They believe in a sense of harmony and non-conflict. They are some of the most compassionate beings on the planet, and they are able to empathize greatly with other people.

This means that sixes are very well-suited to pursue career paths like nurses, pediatricians, counselors, and attorneys. Sixes are prone to volunteer themselves to help others out whenever there is a need. This means that many volunteers fall into this category.

Number sevens are deep thinkers and cogitators. They consider and analyze scenarios much more than any of the other numbers. This precise mentality makes them very diligent in whatever they choose to do. It is also understood that sevens have a natural healing ability that can help themselves and others.

Sevens work excellently at helping others solve their problems and giving them guidance on how to fix certain situations or dilemmas. Sevens should seek career paths that require them to think, analyze, and help others. Detectives, social workers, psychics, and numerologists usually fall into this category.

Number eights are some of the most ambitious people on this list and are very likely to succeed in whatever they put their minds to. With that said, they are more prone to succeed in areas of business because they move through ranks faster than others.

There are, of course, other possibilities that they can consider. Careers in finance, medicine, pharmacy, law, stock trading, and surgery are all career paths that eights excel at. Because of how ambitious eights are, they can be successful in whatever field they find

NUMEROLOGY MADE EASY

themselves in. Because of this, eights should pursue a path that appeals to them, because they will most likely be successful regardless of what they choose.

Number nines are very in touch with nature and are very sympathetic beings. Combined with their abilities to heal others and their vast creativity, they make for very interesting people to befriend.

Nines keep humanity as one of their most important priorities and are always available to volunteer themselves to help others or a greater cause. Nines make excellent writers, civil rights activists, social workers, legal researchers, and musicians.

NUMEROLOGY MADE EASY

Finding Your Number for Luck

https://www.pexels.com/photo/person-about-to-catch-four-dices-1111597/

Understanding your lucky number will enable you to know how to make the best out of certain situations with increased chances of reaping several benefits. Once you know what number you are, you need to also understand what type of luck is associated with your specific life path number.

Number ones are prone to finding luck at the beginning of new ordeals. This allows them to take command of certain situations and lead others when they need to be led. Ones are luckier in business ventures but not necessarily in gaining financial benefits from these ventures.

They are also not the luckiest when it comes to romance and love. However, this does not mean that they won't find someone to love; they may just have a harder time doing so.

Number twos are prone to finding luck when they meditate often and use diplomacy to avoid conflicts. They find that compromising is the best way to solve problems and conflicts. Twos are also the most likely to find solutions when there are issues in larger groups. Even though there will be some compromise, twos are generally lucky in finding an overall solution.

Number threes are some of the luckiest in the whole group. They experience true fortune on a regular basis. This is why the number three is often seen to be lucky by many people. Threes experience luck in situations that need them to be original or creative. They manage to come up with solutions that others normally cannot.

Even though threes are prone to luck, they must still be cautious and avoid taking unnecessary risks in life. Some people think it's wise to bet all of their savings on the three at the roulette table or on the number three horse. This is not prudent, and it may cost one gravely. Try to experience luck associated with threes when you don't expect it.

Number fours experience luck when they want to maintain traditions or come up with new ideas. Both of these scenarios open the door for fours to experience a fair amount of luck. Fours tend to experience fortune with their love lives and are likely to have very stable relationships in their lives. Fours are also likely to provide a stable environment for a business project or another person to grow in.

Number fives are almost as lucky as threes. This means that they will experience fortunate and lucky outcomes in most of the situations that they encounter. This luck extends into some risky ventures because the luck may pay off in the end.

Fives are also fortunate when it comes to romance and love since they are more confident in this area of their lives.

Number sixes are lucky when it comes to their homes and anything that they decide to nurture. This is very helpful for people who are wanting their homes to thrive, but they aren't considered lucky in cases of finance and other business ventures.

NUMEROLOGY MADE EASY

This doesn't mean that sixes will ultimately fail due to financial losses, but they aren't prone to experiencing luck in their finances, either. Fortunately, they are one of the luckiest when it comes to romance and love and often experience rather fortuitous circumstances when pursuing a love interest.

Number sevens do experience luck in their endeavors, but they experience the most of it when it comes to their spiritual growth. This means that luck associated with sevens can be difficult to physically experience because it occurs at a cosmic level. However, that does not mean that it doesn't happen; you may just have to wait a little while to experience the fortunate outcomes.

Number eights are exceptionally lucky when it comes to business. This includes financial gains over the course of one's journey, but it doesn't mean that there won't be some failures along the way. Keep in mind that luck plays in when it needs to.

Eights are the luckiest when it comes to ventures in business, but there can be some cases where these ventures don't seem to work out. This is necessary for eights to keep an attitude that doesn't give up for them to experience all of the benefits of this type of luck.

Number nines are also considered very lucky in all areas of their lives. Some numerologists believe that nine is even luckier than three because nine is three squared. Nines do tend to experience a lot of luck in most aspects of their lives.

Solving Your Number for Your Relationships

https://www.pexels.com/photo/couple-while-holding-hands-691045/

NUMEROLOGY MADE EASY

Unlike other life path numbers that you can solve using the letters in your names, the numbers regarding successful relationships are based on the day that you were born. Your date of birth can help you choose which partner(s) will be suitable for you in the long run.

Number ones are born on the first, tenth, nineteenth, or twenty-eighth of any month. Ones are known to always want to lead, and relationships are no exception to this rule. When ones are truly in love, they will fight for the relationship that they are in and not give up easily. Ones share excellent chemistry with people who are twos or sevens.

Ones do not get along so well with other ones, fives, or sixes. Pursuing a relationship with one of these numbers can result in a painful disaster.

Number twos are born on the second, eleventh, twentieth, or twenty-ninth of any month. Twos are generally very sensitive people and can have a range of different emotions in a small period of time. Twos are known to be both sensual and moody most of the time. Twos are very loyal and don't part easily from people to whom they have made attachments.

It is best for twos to pursue relationships with ones, threes, sevens, eights, and nines as they share the best

NUMEROLOGY MADE EASY

chemistry with these numbers. It is better for twos to avoid long-term relationships with other twos and fours, because they don't usually fit well together.

Number threes are born on the third, twelfth, twenty-first, or thirtieth of any month. Threes are very similar to ones in regards to relationships and will pursue the person that they are in love with whole-heartedly. However, they are very practicality-orientated, and because of that, they aren't prone to follow their hearts when pursuing a relationship with someone.

Threes are generally attracted to sevens, but these types of relationships tend to have many highs and lows. This results in a rather unstable relationship that can lead to a disastrous end. Threes are best suited for relationships with nines, but they can still have healthy relationships with ones, fours, and eights. It is better for threes to avoid getting involved with sixes and sevens, because it can create problems later on in the relationship

Number fours are born on the fourth, thirteenth, twenty-second, or thirty-first of any month. Fours are strangely unconventional since they don't really possess any striking or unique characteristics. Fours are generally more flirtatious beings but are very committed to their relationships when they start them.

With that said, fours aren't the luckiest when it comes to relationships and marriage. They can struggle to find the right life partner, so compatibility testing is absolutely necessary here. Ones and sixes are best suited for fours and can still have healthy relationships with threes, fives, and sevens. Fours should avoid relationships with twos, other fours, eights, and nines to prevent heartbreak along the way.

Number fives are born on the fifth, fourteenth, or twenty-third of any month. Fives are generally known to have many relationships before they get married because they are in the pursuit of finding the perfect match. Fives are also known to get bored with their partners as they become tired of them and want something new or more entertaining.

Fives are best suited to pursue eights since they fit together very well. They have undeniable sexual attraction and are both equally entertaining to one another. Fives can also have healthy relationships with threes, fours, sixes, and nines, but they should avoid pursuing relationships with ones, twos, and other fives.

NUMEROLOGY MADE EASY

Number sixes are born on the sixth, fifteenth, or twenty-fourth of any month and are known as the number of Venus. Venus is known as the planet of peace and love, which means that sixes are drawn to pursuing romantic relationships. Sixes are normally magnetic and charming which boosts their self-confidence during flirtatious encounters.

Sixes are the most compatible with nines, but they can also have healthy and loving relationships with twos, threes, fours, fives, other sixes, and eights. They should avoid ones and sevens. Because of the large number of groups that sixes are compatible with, they are very likely to find a permanent love interest earlier on in life.

Number sevens are born on the seventh, sixteenth, or twenty-fifth of any month. Sevens aren't prone to talk a lot and may even seem distant on romantic dates. However, this is not always the case, because sevens are constantly thinking, which means that they often dream of the future - even a future with the person that they are on a date with.

Because of the quieter temperament of sevens, they are generally drawn to more talkative types. This means that sevens are best suited to ones, twos, and sixes. There are also possibilities with fours, fives, and other sevens, but they should avoid relationships with eights and nines.

Number eights are born on the eighth, seventeenth, or twenty-sixth of any month. Eights are known to be very emotional beings but do maintain a sense of strength and security within themselves. Eights are probably the most loyal of all the numbers and tend to suffer the most heartbreak as they are the most misunderstood. This means that many of their relationships are ended by the partners of eights because they don't fully understand them.

Eights are best suited and most understood by fives, so they should try and pursue a relationship with these numbers. There are other potential successful relationships with ones, twos, sixes, threes, and sevens, but eights should completely avoid fours, other eights, and nines.

Number nines are related to Mars, which is known as a destructive planet in some circles. Nines are born on the ninth, eighteenth, or twenty-seventh of any month. They are filled with energy and underlying aggression. Nines can be emotional, but they tend to hide this part of themselves from the rest of the world around them.

They are prone to end relationships because of their more aggressive temperaments. Nine also tend to want to keep up a tough exterior. As such, they are better off in relationships with numbers that understand their temperaments and who will fight for the ultimate success of the relationship.

This is why nines are best suited for relationships with ones, twos, fives, sevens, and other nines. Because of the emotional temperaments of fours and eights, nines should avoid relationships with these groups.

Solving Your Number for Your Home and Environment

NUMEROLOGY MADE EASY

https://www.pexels.com/photo/home-real-estate-106399/

The home that you move into will have a story (unless you have built your home from scratch). However, your home also has a specific and innate personality that you will need to put some effort into so that you can use numerology to unlock it. Since numbers can relate closely to past events, the address on your house can tell a very specific story.

To find your house's number, all you need to do is add up the digits in the address, if it contains many digits. Add them and work them out according to the same principles that you used for your other life path numbers. If the address is only a single digit, then you have your number.

NUMEROLOGY MADE EASY

If you have letters in your address, then you can use the same model in Chapter 4 to convert the letters to numbers, and after this, you can add them to the number of your address to solve for the right number.

Once you have solved your house's number, you can start to look into the personality and character of your home.

Number ones can be defined as a home filled with strength, innovation, and independence. Homes that are ones are perfect for people who are either single or self-employed. This is because the energy in the home encourages people to be independent and relatively free within themselves and the ways that they think.

It is understood that if you would prefer a warm and cozy home filled with family vibes, then this is not going to be the most conducive of places to live in.

Number twos are homes that are much cozier, warmer, more inviting, and more sensitively-orientated. These homes are completely opposite those that are ones. It has the type of energy that promotes loving relationships, and it creates a sense of harmony between people who are living there.

NUMEROLOGY MADE EASY

If you are a person who loves being around family and loved ones and hanging tons of pictures on the walls, then this is the perfect type of house for you. The energy of it seems to grow when intimate gatherings are celebrated or affectionate emotions are shared between people.

Number threes are homes that generally have a more entertaining type of energy. It is perfect for people who are more creative and upbeat. Any person who relies strongly on creative vibrations in order to be productive will benefit from living in a home like this.

It is perfect for people who want to host fun dinner parties and entertaining social gatherings on a regular basis. However, this type of energy can be dangerous, because it can cause people to become less frugal, more unfocused, and more scattered than previously noticed.

Number fours are homes that create a very grounded feel. Their energies are practical and protected. This type of home creates the types of environments where one wants to be more disciplined and structured in their everyday lives. It is a great place to start a business or family as it accentuates one's feelings of responsibility. With that said, this type of home isn't all serious.

NUMEROLOGY MADE EASY

Because of the different types of grounded energies that it gives off, it does normally allow very abundant gardens to thrive in or around them. Having an indoor or outdoor garden is a great way to maximize the effects of positive energy flow.

Number fives are homes that give off very dynamic energies that allow very positive and active social interactions. These homes have vibrant energies that run deep and create lovely atmospheres for people who like to entertain others. However, it is important to remember that the number five promotes change and variety, which means that you might not be living at that current address for a long time.

These homes aren't ideal for people who enjoy stability and quiet reflections, but they do help people learn important life lessons along the way.

Number sixes are homes that promote loving energies that are experienced in healthy families. This is the type of home where everyone feels welcome. Children and animals thrive in environments with this type of energy. This is the type of home where everyone is just happy to be, even those who don't actually live there.

NUMEROLOGY MADE EASY

There are some setbacks to having a home with this type of energy, the main one being that it can prevent people from venturing out into the world.

With a home like this, it's much nicer to stay in its cocoon of safety and comfort. It sometimes takes a conscious effort to get out for a while.

Number sevens are homes that promote an introspective and reflective type of energy. This is the same energy that allows for spiritual awareness and growth, and it is private and can be considered as rather secretive in many cases. This energy allows for deep thoughts and spiritual reflections.

The number seven home is perfect for people who are introverted and would prefer to avoid other people. Writers, scientists, and professors are drawn to homes like these, because they provide a quiet place for them to think and consider whatever problems they need to solve.

Number eights are homes that promote an ambitious type of energy. This allows for prosperity and abundance. Eights are perfect homes for entrepreneurs or career-driven people as they provide the right type of energy to run a business from home. This is the perfect home for people who wish to expand their financial wealth, their positions in the world, their careers, and their personal statuses.

There are some drawbacks to this type of energy, because many people who live here may become workaholics or even spend too much money on their home due to always wanting to upgrade it. A careful balance must be kept when staying in an eight.

Number nines are homes that promote a very compassionate type of energy. It promotes acceptance and a broader love for community. This is the type of energy that everyone loves to associate with, and it seems to attract visits from many people.

The number nine home teaches you a lot about yourself, because it tends to make people more charitable. The palpable energy of selflessness and charity seems to affect people living here, but that is a positive aspect of nines. People that live in these homes really do want to make the world a better place.

Solving Your Number for Your Health

NUMEROLOGY MADE EASY

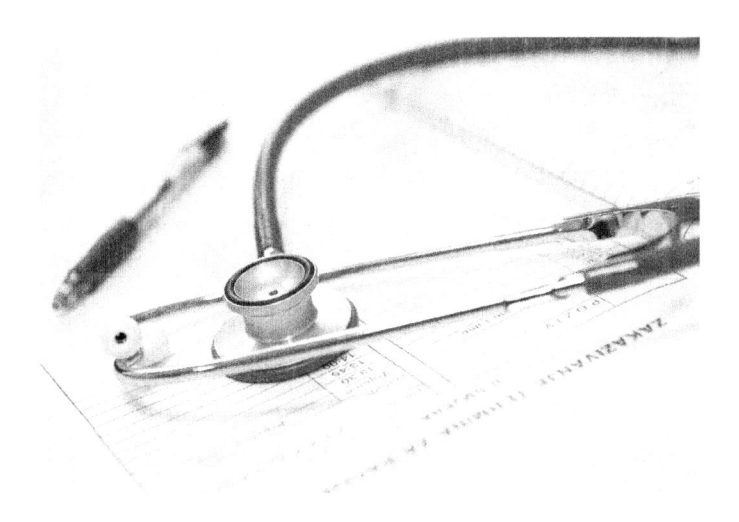

https://www.pexels.com/photo/blue-and-silver-stetoscope-40568/

Unlike other aspects of the numerology numbering system, certain numbers are more prone to certain health ailments instead of benefits. These aspects are noted because they are important to check up with on a regular basis so you can avoid future problems.

Number ones are natural-born leaders, but with this type of leadership quality comes a fair amount of anxiety. This can result in physical effects like the development of heart and kidney problems because of an increase in blood pressure. Ones are also prone to struggling with issues like stress, insomnia, and low self-esteem (even though they act with a lot of confidence).

NUMEROLOGY MADE EASY

Number twos are more aggressive than other people and can have issues with insomnia, other sleep disorders, and short tempers. Because of the tempers that are associated with these numbers, twos tend to be more susceptible to a range of health problems. Some of these include head, circulatory, respiratory, and digestive issues.

Number threes are lucky in most areas of their lives, but they aren't the most fortunate when it comes to avoiding health ailments. Threes don't usually suffer from anxiety or sleep problems like ones and twos, because they don't have the same stressful qualities that precipitate head problems. Threes are more prone to developing diseases associated with their skin, kidneys, nervous systems, and blood.

Number fours often develop general ailments. The energy that is associated with fours seems to affect their immune systems negatively and can make them more susceptible to respiratory infections like colds and influenza. There are also several cases of fours developing problems with their circulation to their extremities.

Because of the slightly more negative energy associated with fours, they more often develop depression later on in life.

NUMEROLOGY MADE EASY

Number fives are likely to develop mental problems because they take much more mental strain than the other numbers. This mental pressure that they experience is much more likely to result in these individuals developing anxiety problems later on in life. It is recommended that fives spend time practicing yoga and meditation to alleviate some of the mental pressure that could be causing them problems.

Fortunately, fives are among the physically healthiest of all the numbers. These overall healthy individuals normally only struggle with problems associated with the kidneys and skin.

Number sixes are very similar to threes because of their decreased immunity. They are more prone to developing respiratory infections from colds and influenza. There is also some chance of developing problems with the nervous system. However, fortunately, sixes aren't prone to suffering from mental or emotional disorders.

Number sevens are normally quite anxious people, which can worsen anxiety problems or other medical conditions if they constantly stress about them. Sevens are prone to developing issues associated with fevers, the cardiovascular system, and the skin. Because of the anxiety that sevens experience on a regular basis, they are more likely to develop problems associated with stress, which can impact their lives negatively.

They will need to find healthy ways to alleviate their stress on a regular basis, such as by practicing yoga and meditation.

Number eights are prone to head, ear, and liver problems. The head problems that afflict eights are generally more physical than mental. Headaches and migraines are common complaints from eights. These can be caused by stress, food sensitivities, or other health problems.

Number nines are prone to developing problems associated with their respiratory systems, kidneys, throats, and muscles of the back and neck. Generally, they don't struggle with emotional or mental problems like most of the other numbers do.

Since all the numbers are prone to some sort of ailments, it is important to regularly check up on the areas that may afflict you. If you know that you are a certain number, then you may be more likely to experience certain problems. This means that, because you know what may affect you, you can start addressing these issues before they set in.

NUMEROLOGY MADE EASY

Some of the health problems can be associated with physical problems and food allergies. If you have a decreased immunity, then boost it with natural supplements and meditation. If you know that your number is more prone to mental and emotional problems, then find healthy ways to deal with them now before they become a problem in the future.

Chapter 9: Numerology Everyday

https://www.pexels.com/photo/white-and-black-weekly-planner-on-gray-surface-1059383/

Numbers are part of our world whether we like it or not. So, how can we consciously tap into their potential and manifest the life we desire? You can, of course, use a numerology chart to learn more about number cycles and patterns in your own life. A good way to start enriching your experience of numbers is simply by becoming more aware of them in your life.

NUMEROLOGY MADE EASY

Do you notice any recurring numerals appearing over and over again in your day-to-day life? If you focus on significant dates in your life, do you notice a pattern?

It was described earlier how names carry vibrations in a similar way that numbers do. So far, we have only dealt with the personal name and what it could mean for you. However, this is not to say that other names should be considered meaningless. On the contrary, all letters of the alphabet carry energetic vibrations.

Thus, the name of your newborn baby, your beloved pet, or your business all send out a certain frequency to the world. Numerology allows you to harness the power of intention and consciously choose exactly what energy you want your loved ones or your creations to emit. So, ask yourself this: What reality do I want these extensions of myself to create?

The same applies to new names that we create for ourselves, for example, through marriage. If, for example, you are considering taking on your husband's surname or a new name that is more suitable for your personality, you can work out the number for this name and see what vibration it has before you make the commitment to do so.

NUMEROLOGY MADE EASY

Although a home itself contains specific energies independent of the number that it has, house numbers also have a particular vibration that can influence its energy, as we have already discussed.

Let us briefly explore, on a more specific level, how you can apply numerology to your life. Remember that we said earlier that the birth name and date are known to represent certain qualities. (We will explore exactly what these characteristics might mean later in this book.) The point here is that changing your own name, or using numerology to name your newborn, for example, can help you set positive intentions and create the life, for you or your baby, that you desire.

Changing your own name using the alchemy of numbers is believed to change your life path. Or, you can look at your last birthday to establish a theme or intention for the current year. Numerology can help us develop healthier relationships, take a more heart-centered approach to our choice of work, and better manage our finances in a more effective manner.

As you can see, numerology can be utilized to address particular questions or challenges that you have had for years, perhaps. However, it can also be adopted as a more integral part of your life and give you a different story by which you can define that very life -

one that involves an intimate relationship between the outer world and your deep and introspective inner self.

The playground of numerology can extend beyond even the borders of your personal life and current lifetime. Through numbers, you can tap into the energies of the wider local and global communities and the planet, even taking a closer look at the karma you have brought with you from various past lifetimes.

In the narrative of contemporary modern society, we are conditioned to automatically walk the one-way street toward material success, longevity, and wealth. It's more of a cold and deserted superhighway than an unassuming country road framed with well-intentioned, friendly neighbors and littered with the hopes and dreams of a better future.

Chapter 10: Developing Your Intuition

Although most of us don't know it, we all have the ability to be intuitive. It is an integral part of who we are as humans. Exploring the different ways that our intuitive gifts can manifest is well beyond the scope of this book, but we are all familiar with that feeling of having a hunch. Often, our daily decisions are not based on following such inklings, especially those who have a tendency to dwell in the realms of the mind.

It is fascinating to watch the synchronicity of birds in flight: Without conscious deliberation, they coordinate themselves intuitively. We, like them, have the potential to tap into this primal knowledge that transcends the most insistent of minds if we allow ourselves to cut through the incessant mental chatter. If there is one thing that we can learn from the mystical arts, it is that there is more to reality than meets the eye.

Tapping into a wider consciousness can help us to feel more confident and more connected, and it is waiting for you to allow it to reveal its magic.

How to Strengthen Your Intuition

https://www.pexels.com/photo/fire-orange-emergency-burning-1749/

Setting your intention to become more intuitive is a powerful way to start. There are a few simple activities you can do to help you exercise the muscle of your intuition. Like anything else that you want to master, doing so requires practice and patience.

First, make it a point of spending some quiet time alone every day. Living in the 21st century can sometimes feel like a tug-of-war with our emotions, thoughts, and even our bodies. It's not called the rat race for no reason - we can sometimes feel like we are on a hamster wheel, pursuing destinations that never give us the sense of completion we desperately long for.

The neon lights and alluring promises of the next best thing may be tempting, but they can have the effect of bombarding us with a sensory overload that inhibits us from accessing our inner resources.

Spending time alone, preferably in nature, is an act of self-care that can mysteriously, and sometimes instantaneously, transport us from the chaos of modern-day life to a profound stillness that helps us to connect to the natural world and dimensions within ourselves that can often feel unreachable.

Second, pay attention to your feelings and mood. Humans can be highly receptive to other energies. If you practice being more attuned to recognizing how you are feeling and suddenly experience an unexpected emotion, you may be picking up on other people's feelings. When this happens, ask yourself if it is genuinely how you are feeling and why. If there is no apparent reason, you should be able to let it go. This will enable you to develop the inner strength to move through the often-overwhelming stream of energy we receive from our world.

Being able to differentiate between your own emotions and those of others also helps to develop a greater sense of awareness of your environment, thereby shutting down your mind. If you do notice emotions such as fear pop up unexpectedly, it could be telling you something about the intentions of others. In this way, this exercise can help you develop your ability to intuitively recognize and respond to dangerous situations, for example.

Third, at the beginning of the day, ask yourself a question you don't know the answer to, and do not Google it. In fact, don't rely on any outside source to provide you with the answer. Without forcing it, simply pay attention to what comes up. Listen to your inner self, and be aware of what is going on around you. You may be surprised at what you find. We are part of an infinite pool of knowledge through spirit or the collective unconscious; it is a matter of learning how to allow ourselves to tap into it.

NUMEROLOGY MADE EASY

Fourth, don't overthink! Most of us tend to revert to the default setting of overthinking when we are faced with a choice. Even the best of us can sometimes get caught up in the cognitive gymnastics of the mind without meaning to. Make a conscious decision to go with your gut when you are faced with choices. Allow yourself to follow your heart in regards to dealing with challenges, responses, and decisions, and follow through to see where it takes you.

Finally, be aware of numbers. You now understand how influential they can be in your life. If you know how to read and understand them, you will be able to use that knowledge to your advantage.

Conclusion

In this book, we have explored an approach to numbers that has exposed them as an intrinsic ingredient in the beautiful alchemy of everything - as the blueprint for the present and the future. Mathematics is the language used to represent numbers. Numbers hold potential for creation. If we could treat our own lives as having the same spectrum of infinite possibilities at our fingertips, we could truly manifest the realities we desire.

Numerology is one tool that enables us to do this. You have learned that, according to the ancient wisdom of numbers, they provide a means by which we can notice patterns in our lives. If we pay attention to them, we can use the lessons from the patterns of the past to help us better navigate the waters of troubled relationships and other challenges we face.

We also covered some of the ways in which numbers can be of value in your everyday life. You can be more aware of and better understand the number patterns in your life. You were introduced to an arsenal of methods you used to work out significant numbers in your life, such as the life path number and your birthday number.

NUMEROLOGY MADE EASY

You can use this guidebook in the future to help you apply numerological methods as a way of life - a way of interpreting what is going on around you and defining recurring themes and challenges you face. No matter what your level of understanding of numerology was when you started reading this book, you should now be well-equipped to apply your greater understanding of numbers in your life. Hopefully, by reading this book, you will have gained another perspective of yourself and, therefore, more self-knowledge.

As you complete this journey, it is hoped that you step out into the world with a greater appreciation of numbers as the fabric of the world. If you can cut through your mental chatter and start to see the subtle patterns that whisper to you through cycles, you are starting down a path of self-healing, empowerment, and growth that is in tune with the divine harmony of nature.

We hope that you have gathered that, as sure as the sun will rise again tomorrow, numbers can help you navigate your world and create a more heart-centered life that takes its rightful place in the great symphony of the universe. If you can shrug off the burden of the linear way of thinking that we have inherited, you can start walking more lightly through the world with a greater sense of peace.

Creation and destruction are a cycle that governs our lives. Anything that grows in an environment that provides it with the perfect conditions for it to flourish will seek further growth; and as living beings, it is part of our nature to create.

We build empires, make music, procreate, and we construct homes. We have even engineered rockets to send people to the moon. And so it can be said that the ultimate work of art - the ultimate act of creation - is our life. We are creating reality anyway, whether we are conscious of it or not, but we have the power to create consciously.

This is the beginning of your new journey. Enjoy it as you use this freshly-gained knowledge in numerology to make certain life decisions and transform various parts of yourself. This was just an introduction to numerology; there is still a lot more to learn. Don't let the lesson end here. Now that you know the basics, you can start diving into much deeper aspects of numerology.

NUMEROLOGY MADE EASY

Bluesource And Friends

This book is brought to you by Bluesource And Friends, a happy book publishing company.

Our motto is **"Happiness Within Pages"**

We promise to deliver amazing value to readers with our books.

We also appreciate honest book reviews from our readers.

Connect with us on our Facebook page www.facebook.com/bluesourceandfriends and stay tuned to our latest book promotions and free giveaways.

References

Anderson, E. [Earl Anderson]. (2018, May 9). *Understanding numerology: the basics on finding out your numbers, numerology 101 for beginners* [Video]. YouTube. https://www.youtube.com/watch?v=zV8nuwfwxxk

Buchanan, M. (2015). Numerology: Discover Your Future, Life Purpose and Destiny From Your Birth Date and Name. Hay House Basics.

Ducie, S. (1999). The Complete Illustrated Guide to Numerology: Using the Language of Numbers as a Personal Life Guide. Element Books.

Ducie, S. [Kris Meredith]. (2020, May 26). *Numerology Explained with Sonja Ducie*[Video]. YouTube. https://www.youtube.com/watch?v=SKU1hcVsago.

Ducie, S. [watkinsbooks]. (2015, July 25). *Numerology explained by Sonia Ducie* [Video]. YouTube. https://www.youtube.com/watch?v=Ra1CdL7eajE

ETimes. (2018, December 2017). *Love Numerology Numbers: Find Your Partner as per Numerology.* Entertainment Times. https://timesofindia.indiatimes.com/life-style/relationships/love-sex/Find-your-partner-as-per-numerology/articleshow/16850388.cms

Ghosh, A. [InnerWorldRevealed-Numerology and More]. (2019, April 24). *Numerology - The Four Different Systems -*

NUMEROLOGY MADE EASY

Chaldean, Kabbalah, Vedic, Pythagorean [Video]. YouTube. https://www.youtube.com/watch?v=gUqI3c6ctOI

Hurst, K. (n.d). *Numerology: What Is Numerology and How Does It Work?* The Laws of Attraction by Greater Minds. https://www.thelawofattraction.com/what-is-numerology/

Lightheart, C. (2017). Numerology for Beginners: Numerology Foundations, Secret Meaning of Numbers in Your Life, Insight and Guidance Toward Life Mastery. Maplewood Publishing.

[Numerology Explained]. (2020, June 9). *What is Numerology? - Numerology Explained for Beginners - Numerology Basics - Numerology History* [Video]. YouTube. https://www.youtube.com/watch?v=oLWyIDmQlRw

[Numerology Secrets]. (2015, May 4). *Chaldean Numerology For Beginners* [Video]. YouTube. https://www.youtube.com/watch?v=Og2DKeDANvY

[Numerology Secrets]. (2015, August 19). *Learn Numerology 101 (For Beginners!)* [Video]. YouTube. https://www.youtube.com/watch?v=EL7Ngxpiu28

[Numerology Secrets]. (2015, April 5). *Numerology Explained: What Is Numerology?* [Video]. YouTube. https://www.youtube.com/watch?v=_uDzPEDYRZw

[Numerology Secrets]. (2015, May 28). *Pythagorean Numerology: Intro To Pythagoras Numerology* [Video]. YouTube. https://www.youtube.com/watch?v=AFhnRJEAllQ

NUMEROLOGY MADE EASY

Sethi, S. (2020, January 27). *How Numerology Can Help You to Find the Best Career in 2020.* https://sanjaysethi.org/find-best-career-2020/

Shaha, A. [The Guardian]. (2013, July 9). *Painted with numbers: mathematical patterns in nature* [Video]. YouTube. https://www.youtube.com/watch?v=O7x3LBWn-Ao

Spano, R. [Emory University]. (2010, April 24). *Robert Spano on Kabbalah numerology* [Video]. YouTube. https://www.youtube.com/watch?v=AHc3xQd0WmQ

TED. (2016, December 13). *Maths is the hidden secret to understanding the world|RogerAtonsen|TEDTalks* [Video]. YouTube. https://www.youtube.com/watch?v=ZQElzjCsl9o

VeAstrology. (n.d). *Numerology Lucky Numbers.* http://veastrology.com/lucknumbers.html

Printed in Great Britain
by Amazon